A Little

Bathroom

Book

SUMMERSDALE

Copyright © Summersdale Publishers Ltd 1998

No part of this book may be reproduced by any means,
nor transmitted, nor translated into a machine language
without the written permission of the publisher.

Summersdale Publishers Ltd
46 West Street
Chichester
West Sussex
PO19 1RP
UK

ISBN 1 84024 021 0

Cover design by Java Jive, Chichester

Contents

Introduction

The bathroom is perhaps the most popular room in today's house. A haven of tranquillity and warmth, it is a place not only to get clean but also to relax without interruption.

Over the years the humble bathroom has experienced many changes in accordance with fashion and technological innovation. In ancient Greece the bath was swift, cold and invigorating, whereas the Romans used the bath and bathroom as a place of relaxation and healing, and Turkish baths were built for similar purposes. On the other hand, the European bath was, especially in the eighteenth and early nineteenth centuries, used almost exclusively for medicinal purposes.

Therefore down the centuries the bathroom has been used for relaxation, healing, invigoration and enjoyment. Little has changed to this day – people use the bathroom in their own individual way, whether it is for that cold invigorating shower in the morning or that long relaxing bath in the evening; whether they bathe with company or alone; whether they regard the bathroom as purely functional or as a haven in which to relax and unwind.

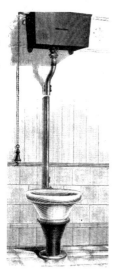

The History of the Bathroom

Although bathrooms were rare in people's homes prior to the twentieth century, the Romans built and maintained elaborate warm public baths, supplying 300 gallons of water per person per day. In 1598, Queen Elizabeth I had a valve water closet fitted in her room. This W.C. was not simply used for decoration, moreover: she wrote in her diary that she used it whether she needed it or not. However, bathing was not available to ordinary families as an activity to take for granted until this century.

Before the advent of indoor plumbing, washing was something of a performance. Water had to be pumped manually and then carried back to the house. Carrying twenty or thirty gallons of water at a time, transferring it to the stove to be heated and then to the tub was no small task and it was no wonder that washing was not to be taken lightly. The father of the family would wash first, followed by the children, going from cleanest to dirtiest. Each would be scrubbed down with harsh handmade soap and rinsed with an additional bucket of water. The mother would wash last. Finally the water had to be discarded, bucket by bucket, out of the back door. Keeping clean was hard work.

By the end of the 19th century, technological developments were moving the bathroom – the sink, the bathtub and the toilet – inside the house. Large cities were developing water supplies – albeit unfiltered and unchlorinated – and sanitary disposal systems, which made this progress possible.

Fortunately, washing is not such a problem for us today. In fact, we take our bathrooms completely for granted. Some homes boast two or three bathrooms, in addition to one for guests. En-suites have become a part of life and modern bathrooms with hot tubs and whirlpool baths have made bathing as much of a social occasion as it was in the Roman era.

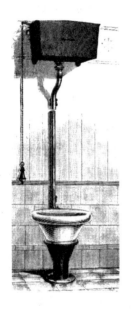

The History of the Toilet

The first flushing toilet was in use over 4,000 years ago (around 1700 BC) in the Palace of Knossos on the island of Crete. However, ancient culture could not get to grips with this contraption, and it was not until over 3500 years later that someone took the matter in hand. In 1596, Sir John Harington of England invented the water closet for his godmother, Queen Elizabeth I – but his efforts were in vain. Mocked and derided for his invention, he only ever made the one model. Subsequently, society lost out, because the first toilet was not introduced for another 200 years.

The dark ages of these toilet-less years can have been no fun at all. Large private houses often boasted a 'privy', a small room like the room that we would call the modern-day toilet – except that there was no toilet inside. Instead, there was a vertical shaft in the wall, sometimes with a seat over it and sometimes not. The shaft would lead into the moat, if it were a castle, or else simply into a pit. It was rumoured that one of the best-paid domestic jobs in these large estates was to rake out the moat. Some prudish types mistook these small rooms for tiny chapels.

Public privies in the cities were made of plain wooden planks and were built over deep pits. These conveniences were not without their dangers – frequently the wood would rot and the unfortunate citizen would fall through the hole into the pit. Drowning in excrement would have been a pretty horrible way to go.

The problem of the toilet-less years was also overcome by a series of chamber pots, ranging from the humblest and primitive of clay jars to the most ornate and finely decorated china vessels. The extent to which the chamber pot was decorated was an indication of one's wealth. Other means included outhouses and pits with a layer of ashes at the bottom. However, while these may have done the trick of waste disposal, it can be imagined that the smell was not particularly sweet and that hygiene was not top of the agenda.

On the subject of hygiene, we owe much to a man called Cummings. Leading a fairly tedious life as a watchmaker, Cummings took it upon himself to take the matter of revolutionising the toilet. Consequently, we have Cummings to thank for odour-less bathrooms. He invented the S-bend, a curved tube of standing water, to prevent unpleasant odours entering the house.

Original toilets were made in two pieces, but in 1885, Thomas Twyford invented a one-piece model without the need of a supporting wooden case. So, the question remains, where does the renowned Thomas Crapper fit into all this? Just his name alone is enough to send toilet enthusiasts into spasms of glee, but it would appear that he is something of a mystery figure. Although he did own a successful plumbing business, he was most definitely not the inventor of the toilet. Plus, the word association that brings his name to mind was around long before he was.

Life before the flushing toilet can hardly have been fun. The crowded and unsanitary living conditions that resulted from mass urbanisation in the last century meant that most families kept a glass or metal jar, which the whole family would then use as a toilet.

When this pot was in danger of overflowing, it would then be emptied out into the street. Whilst depositing human waste in the street was nothing new, the overcrowding in the cities did not create the healthiest of environments. Politeness dictated that if you were about to perform this ritual, it was courtesy to shout out of the window, 'Gardez l'eau' (meaning 'watch out for the water' in French). The British were never great linguists and the British accent made the word 'l'eau' sound like 'loo', which is, of course, still widely in use today.

Toilets also feature extensively in the Bible. King Eglon was killed in the process of 'relieving himself in the inner room of the house' (Judges 3: 24). Jehu destroyed Baal's temple, 'and the people have used it for a latrine to this day' (2 Kings 10: 27).

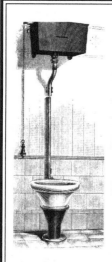

There are passages of Ulysses that can be read only in the toilet if one wants to extract the full flavour from them.

Henry Miller, *Black Spring*

It cannot be denied that Victorian ladies led a somewhat sheltered life. The first time many of them actually experienced a flushing toilet was at the Great Exhibition of 1851. They were quite fascinated as to how such complex apparatus could work and peered below to try and work out the mechanics of it. The reflection of their own behinds offended their Victorian sensibilities, and so patterned bowls became the accepted norm.

Victorian gentlemen were not renowned for their aim. Some stand-up urinals would have a picture of a bee to aim for. All is revealed when it turns out that the Latin for bee is 'apis'.

Toilet Paper

There is no denying that there has always been a need for the stuff; however, it is only relatively recently that it has come into being. Resources and locations dictated how people coped without it, but leaves were a popular solution, and Hawaiians were apparently content to use coconut shells.

However, for the rest of us, less fortunate, mortals, there may have been a distinct lack of handy coconuts. Others living near the sea used mussel shells (ouchhh!) and ancient Roman public bathrooms provided a stick with a sponge attached to the end of it. After the stick had done the honours, it was returned to a bowl of saltwater, ready for the next customer! It is really no wonder that plagues and diseases spread so rapidly. Wealthy Romans used the same principle, but wool was attached to the stick and it was then preserved in rose-water. Louis XIV and other French aristocrats apparently used lace, but that's the French for you.

Before the invention of the printing press, Americans found that corn on the cob made excellent wiping material. However, once newspapers started to be printed and circulated widely, it was discovered that their use was not merely limited to spreading news!

At last, in 1879, the Scott brothers invented toilet paper, as we know it. When it was first produced, it consisted of single squares of coarse paper, which must have been rather like sandpaper, but by the first decade of the 1900s, people were revelling in the soft, fluffy, luxurious paper that we know today. It took some time before the British could cope with seeing it displayed in chemists, who had to sell it from under the counter.

Thankfully the paper that used to be found in schools or public toilets that resembled tracing paper seems to have disappeared.

In India, it is a widely observed 'toiletological' custom never to let the right hand know what the left is in the process of doing. Perhaps the rest of the story is just best left to the imagination.

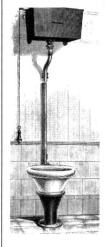

All the major airlines have now installed frosted glass in their toilet windows. This would seem to be taking modesty a little far – the chances of a passing astronaut or UFO peering in are fairly negligible.

And just to dispel the fears of any neurotics out there, any lumps of ice that fall from passing aircraft are coming from the wings, and not the toilets.

Bathroom Habits

Here are some categories into which the human race can be divided on the basis of their bathroom habits:

The Examiner

– who examines the toilet paper after use to determine whether further wiping is required.

The Stander

– who stands up before using the toilet paper to facilitate the general proceedings.

The Hyper-Critical
    – who carefully and neatly folds his toilet paper.

The Don't Care How you Do It
    – who does not carefully or neatly fold his toilet paper.

The Double Taker
    – who uses the same piece of toilet paper more than once.

The Cleanse'n'Purger
> – who urinates in the shower.

The Hand Washer
> – who washes his hands.

The Skanky So-and-So
> – who does not wash his hands.

The Obsessive
> – who gets into the most almighty flap about which way the toilet paper is hung on the spool.

While most of us would not deny ourselves the luxury of answering nature's call, Saint Catherine of Sienna tried to go as little as possible. She 'denied herself daily relief' as a punishment for all the things she had done wrong.

One disgusted writer, it would seem, had little time for the privy: 'Privy houses set against ye Strete which spoiling people's apparill should they happen to be nare when ye filth comes out . . . Especially in ye Night when people cannot see to shun them'.

A book of medieval customs says 'Beware of draught privys and of pyssying in draughts, and permyt no common pyssing place about the house'.

In the year 106, the Saxon king, Edmund Ironside, was murdered while answering a call of nature. A manuscript records that he was 'struck with a spear in the fundament while at the withdraught to purge nature'. Not the most comfortable way to go.

According to recent research carried out in America by teams of researchers lurking in the shadows of public conveniences, only 68% of the population wash their hands after using the toilet.

Some health officials would have it that hand washing is the most important thing a person can do to stay healthy, far surpassing diet and alcohol consumption – which is quite reassuring really, and cheaper than vitamin supplements.

According to the sponsors of 'Operation Clean Hands', however, hand washing is a refined art form. Apparently it's just not worth the hassle unless you use warm or hot running water and anti-bacterial soap, washing the wrists, the palms, the back of the hands, the fingers and under the nails, rubbing the hands together for at least 10-15 seconds. The hands should then be dried from the forearms towards the hands and the fingertips – which is not quite so reassuring.

Harington wrote: 'To keep your houses sweet, cleanse privy vaults: to keep your souls as sweet, mend privy fault'.

Bathing

Bathing has been a prominent part of life ever since the most ancient history. Religion, sex and medicine have all put bathing in an important position. Homer tells of the gods and goddesses of ancient Greece taking baths as preparation for seduction. The Romans introduced public baths, which then developed into huge centres of gratification in all senses of the word – where the hot water and steaming vapours gave birth to scented sensuality.

As time went by, frequenters of the baths stopped even pretending that they were going for academic or athletic purposes – their motives were no longer purely platonic. Although men and women were strictly separated, slaves and masseurs of the opposite sex were used and the French writer Montaigne writes that it was the custom for ladies to 'receive men in the vapour baths' for steamy entertainment.

After Rome's decline, the unsupervised baths became holes of depravity. Christians, who had worked to build the baths, denounced them as heathen works. The buildings fell into disrepair and were abandoned.

While public baths were on the wane in Europe, the Middle East had caught onto the trend and hundreds of them were built there. Moreover, there is evidence that some Roman baths built in the northern regions of the Roman Empire continued to operate, and mixed bathing parties provided the opportunity for German friends to see each other socially throughout the Middle Ages. Apparently, 'Everyone undressed at home and went to the baths practically naked . . . The men went into the baths wearing a suspendory; on their entering, an attendant handled them a bundle of rods, intended for massage; the women's bathing costume consisted of a diminutive apron which usually slipped off the hips. The bathers had to be attended to by members of the opposite sex'.

There was no sexual segregation, the customers mingled openly and freely and the erotic atmosphere of these medieval German baths rivalled those of the Romans. In the end, they became little more than public brothels, where emphasis was less on hygiene than on sexual games.

Baths became centres of fashion. Fashionable ladies expressed their femininity in ornate head-dresses, whilst both men and women wore hats in the bath. In private houses, beds were provided in curtained alcoves, musicians were employed to serenade the bathers and one manuscript shows a group of gay Gothic couples partaking of a buffet supper served from a table set up in a large communal tub.

England and France came to realise the delights of communal bathing during the Crusades, when English knights discovered the pleasures of the Islamic bath. Indeed, the Order of the Bath is supposed to have originated from the young virgins who delighted the knight while he was in the bath. One manuscript even portrays a knight relaxing in his bath surrounded by a whole host of young females showering him with rose petals.

Before the Crusades, the English attitude to water was one of wariness. It was dangerous to drink unless it had been 'cleansed and pourged by boylynge', for it was believed to be 'infect with frogges and other wormes that brede'. Pure springs and holy wells were used primarily for healing purposes and were closely guarded by monks and friars.

> *Wine, women, baths, by art or Nature warm,*
> *Used and abused do men much good or harm.*

This message, contained in a Latin manuscript on cleanliness, was given to William the Conqueror's son, Robert, by the doctors of Salerno in 1096. However, once bathing gained popularity, public baths earned the reputation of being *Seminaria Venenata*, or seminaries of sex and sensuality.

Many women claimed that bathing in water used by a man had made them pregnant and 'frogges and other wormes' of fertility were feared to inhabit male bath water, despite Sir Thomas Browne's 12th century assurances, that it was impossible to 'fornicate at a distance'.

Soon, following Continental tradition, the English baths became centres of prostitution and depravity. The word 'stewhouse' was used for either a public bath or a brothel, just as in the Italian, 'bagnio' was used to indicate either. While the upper classes enjoyed more privacy at home and usually had private baths fitted, couples would still often bathe together. If they were caught, they would claim that it was all in the interests of saving water, a major concern when it had to be purchased by the bucketful or else hauled by hand from the town pump.

By the end of the 15th century, however, Europe was stricken by plagues and the public baths started to be closed as possible culprits. Max von Boehn, a German student of manners described that 'ladies and gentlemen of the 16th century arrayed themselves in the most costly fabrics; they were stiff with velvets, silks and gold brocades; they were positively plastered with pearls and precious stones; and . . . they stank like the plague!'

Bath twice a day to be really clean, once a day to be passably clean, once a week to avoid being a public menace.

Anthony Burgess, *Mr Enderby*

Bertrand Russell wrote of 'nuns who never take a bath without wearing a bathrobe all the time. When asked why, since no man can see them, they reply "Oh, but you can't forget the good God"'.

Roman Baths

The remains of the ancient Roman baths that are left to us today give substantial evidence that bathing was an absolutely central part of Roman culture. Built to an efficient design, the baths provided an active social forum.

The public baths would usually consist of five main parts, comprising the *apodyterium*, the *palaestra*, the *caldarium*, the *tepidarium* and the *frigidarium*. The *apodyterium* was a changing room where the bather could leave personal possessions. The *frigidarium*, *tepidarium* and *caldarium* were baths containing cold, warm and hot water respectively. The order in which the Romans visited these individual baths was a matter of preference. The *palaestra* was a central outdoor yard for exercise, usually surrounded by columns. Unlike Greek baths, this was not a location to exercise seriously, but rather to socialise and relax.

Ancient Roman baths will always be associated with a luxuriance that we may find hard to imagine. After visiting Herculaneum several times, Seneca stated, 'We think ourselves poor and mean if our walls [of the baths] are not resplendent with large and costly mirrors; if our marbles [statues and busts] are not set off by mosaics of Numidian stone, or their borders are not faced over on all sides with different patterns, arranged in many colours like paintings; if our vaulted ceilings are not buried in glass; if our swimming pools are not lined with Thasian marble, once a rare and wonderful sight in any temple; and finally, if the water has not been poured from silver spigots'.

A private bathroom of the wealthy consisted of a pool of water, and was, essentially, a small swimming pool. The walls were lined with marble as were the three or four marble steps leading down to the submerged floor. Both the water and the air were heated and the entire floor rested on pillars of bricks that drew hot air from an adjacent furnace. The bath had a plug and the water would be emptied once or twice a day.

We may be concerned about ecology and wasting water, but compared to our Roman ancestors, it wouldn't seem that we are doing too badly at all. The people of ancient Rome used about 1,300 litres of water a day in their baths and their toilets, which is almost six times as much as Londoners use today.

Save water –
bath with a friend

Semi-official slogan, UK, from the mid-1970s

It was said that Queen Elizabeth I was remarkably advanced for her time in matters of hygiene. Indeed, she was in the habit of taking a bath once a month — 'whether she needed it or not'.

Bathrooms in Ancient Egypt

Not only did the homes of the rich in ancient Egypt boast bedrooms, servants' quarters, halls and dining rooms, they also had bathrooms. A 'bathroom' was a small recessed room with a slab of limestone in the corner. The master of the house would stand in regal splendour on the slab while his slaves would douse him with water. The waste-water ran into a large bowl in the floor below or through an earthenware channel in the wall where it emptied into yet another bowl outside. This bowl was then baled out by hand.

The Japanese Bathroom

While public baths have all but died out in the Western world, this institution is an integral part of Japanese life. The public bath is called the 'sento' and is identified by its 23 metre high chimney. The most important thing about the Japanese bath is that the bathtub is not actually for washing. It is first for warming the body and then for relaxing the tired muscles and nerves. It is expected that you wash the most obviously dirty parts of your body before entering the tub. A basin and a small stool are provided for this purpose. Public bathhouses have two baths, 'quite hot' and 'hot' – both are scented.

The Japanese domestic bath is also different from Western norms. Similar to the public baths, you are supposed to wash outside of the bath. No soap should enter the bathing water. The tub is filled with water and everyone in the house uses the same bath water. Therefore, it is a matter of courtesy to keep the water clean. The temperature of the bath is usually far hotter than Westerners are used to – apparently the hotter the water, the more relaxed you feel afterwards. The bath itself is square and much deeper than a Western bath.

Traditional Japanese toilets are considered to be cleaner than Western ones, because no part of the body can come into contact with it. For this particular bodily function, squatting is thought to be more hygienic than sitting. Many homes in the countryside still do not have flush toilets, and the 'bakuma-ka' (honey wagon) is not an unfamiliar sight (or smell). Public toilets are all over Japan, but many do not have towels or toilet paper. Hot running water is unusual. The Japanese always carry a handkerchief or tissues around with them for their hands.

But once the traditional 'squatter' has been mastered, the latest generation of Japanese toilet may pose more than a little confusion to the poor unsuspecting foreigner. The three alphabets making up the Japanese language and the new fashion craze of women gluing their bras into place are nothing compared to the intricacies of the modern Japanese toilet that looks as though it comes out of the space age. The control panel is worthy of an aeroplane cockpit. The toilets clean themselves, have germ-resistant coatings and spray pulsating water to massage your behind.

Moreover, the control panel boasts a digital clock that tells you how long you have been in the bathroom. Buttons control the temperature of the water squirted onto your behind. The bottom-washer, complete with bottom-dryer, is meant to do away with the need for toilet paper. Other buttons operate the lid and some even have a hand-held remote control system, not to mention automatic seat warmers.

However, the disadvantages to such a model are not inconsiderable. The control panel can be pretty daunting to novices – nobody relishes the idea of being stranded on a Japanese loo trying to get it to flush. Although, being stranded on a Japanese loo unable to switch off the spraying bidet without drenching oneself and the bathroom would be considerably worse.

Nevertheless, it cannot be denied that Toto, the Japanese toilet manufacturer, goes to great lengths to make its products user-friendly, because, they say, people want to relax in the bathroom. Yojiro Watanabe, speaking for Toto, says that Japanese homes are usually so small and lifestyles have become so frenetic that the bathroom is often the only place where people can be alone.

Bathroom Superstition

Have a bath in between Christmas and New Year's Day and you will remain clean all year.

Getting a towel twisted after using it will bring bad luck.

If you dry your hands with a friend, you will be friends forever.

If you use the water that someone else has washed in, you and that person will have a quarrel.

Never wash your face with soap every day, or hair will grow on your chin

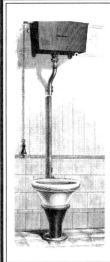

I test my bath before I sit
And I'm always moved to wonderment
That what chills the finger not a bit
Is so frigid on the fundament

Ogden Nash, *Samson Agonistes*

That Greek one is my hero, who watched the bath water rise above his navel and rushed out naked, 'I found it, I found it' into the street in all his shining and forgot that others would only stare at his genitals.
Dannie Abse, Walking Under Water

It is the height of luxury to sit in a hot bath and read about little birds.

Alfred, Lord Tennyson (having had running water installed into his new house at Aldworth)

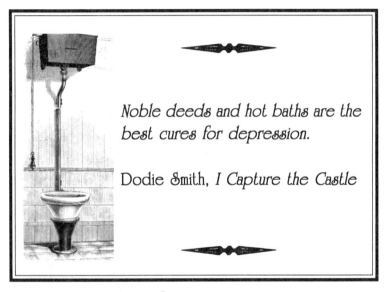

Noble deeds and hot baths are the best cures for depression.

Dodie Smith, *I Capture the Castle*

I have had a good many more uplifting thoughts, creative and expansive visions while soaking in comfortable baths, or drying myself after bracing showers, in well-equipped American bathrooms than I have ever had in any cathedral.

Edmund Wilson, A Piece Of My Mind

In medieval stories of seduction, a couple would begin an evening by taking a bath together. The whole concept of propriety and modesty were completely different from ours. The whole household and their guests would often sleep in one room, with no night-clothes – nudity was not the taboo that it is today, and bathrooms were hence much less private places than they might be today.

Bathing has widespread ritualistic associations. Washing is believed not only to remove dirt, but also invisible stains. A BBC broadcast told how the fishermen of Milford Haven refuse to wash after a good catch for fear of 'washing their luck away'.

In Lapland, three ducklings are annually washed through a hole in the river ice, to bring the community luck for the coming year. Russian babies also had to undergo similar treatment in the River Neva, although it would seem that we can rest assured that this practice has now died out.

Bath Therapy

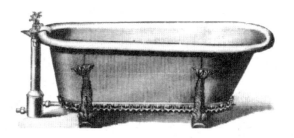

Balneotherapy develops the whole concept of bathing as relaxation and is used to talk about the study of bathing as therapy, and a self-healing cure for disease. The therapy uses entirely natural elements and makes use of hot springs, climatic factors and peat substances. The process works by stimulating the body by soaking in hot water. This both helps pain and improves the general well being of both the body and the mind. This type of treatment is one of the oldest medical procedures known to mankind and has been widely practised in both Europe and Asia.

Peat bathing uses a special blend of minerals and enzymes, which, combined with the heat, helps to improve the circulation and relaxes muscles and tissues. This enhances the immune system and makes the bather feel more alive and invigorated.

You can buy special packs of peat to perform this ritual. Alternatively, if you're feeling hard-up, you could adopt the DIY approach and go excavating in a peat bog.

The Shower

Not wanting to take things for granted, it seems reasonably safe to assume that most of us put washing as a fairly high priority in our daily routine. However, as with everything in modern life, the bathing process has had to be speeded up. A bath is not something that most of us have time for first thing in the morning, and a shower is far more practical. Indeed, even our most ancient ancestors used a primitive kind of shower, standing under natural waterfalls to scrub themselves clean. Those not blessed with a waterfall in their back garden used a bucket of icy cold water to rinse the soap from their bodies.

However, from the start of the 18th century, developments meant that we could enjoy this natural phenomenon in the comfort of our own homes. At first, the shower was regarded with considerable suspicion among the English middle and upper classes, which is not altogether surprising when one considers the appearance of the early models.

The first construction was over 12 feet high, made of metal, painted to look like bamboo and consisted of a basin with a drain at the bottom and a hidden tank on the top which were joined by poles about 10 feet long. This contraption probably resembled a primitive torture instrument. A pump on the lower basin forced water up to the top basin through a hollow pole and then down upon the bather's head. The only problem was that the whole concept of hygiene was somewhat turned on its head, as the same water was used time and time again.

Hinges were attached to the top to support a shower curtain and the bather probably wore some form of shower cap, tall and conical and made from oiled material, which must have been quite some fashion statement. Showering was a long process, as the shower was not an end in itself. After the ablutions, the men would perfume themselves and choose their clothes for the day – which could take hours.

Another early model of shower, developed in America, was called the Virginia Stool Shower. This came into being in the 1830s, was made of walnut, and had a revolving seat. It was placed in a bathtub and a hand-operated lever pumped water up to the bather's head and shoulders. A foot pedal controlled a scrubbing brush, which could be worked up and down the bather's back.

Modern showers as we know them first came into being in the late 1800s. In 1889, the J. L. Mott Iron Works, manufacturers and importers of 'the latest and most approved plumbing appliances for all classes of building', included in its catalogue, its newfangled model with 'needle, shower descending douche, liver spray and bidet bath'. The bather was then covered with warm water from every angle. A network of pipes surrounded the bather, carrying the water to various outlets.

None of the piping was hidden and it formed a shield of privacy around the bather.

The grandness of showers did not last and the norm for showers became the single head. The possibilities for showers were then left until the 1980s, when the introduction of the 'vertical whirlpool' offered the same luxuries as the Mott models had done a century before.

Shower Therapy

Hydropathy is a pseudoscientific method of treating disease using large quantities of water. Vincent Priessnitz, a Silesian peasant was the undisputed inventor of the 'water cure'. His experiments with water to heal his own wounds led to the discovery of its healing properties. Possibly as a result of this, Hydropathic establishments multiplied in the latter half of the nineteenth century, as water was applied to the patient in a growing number of ways to heal a variety of ailments.

The Rain Bath

The patient stood in a shallow brick pit surrounded by a wooden screen. The doctor then operated the tap attached to an overhead nozzle using a cord. This primitive shower arrangement claimed to cure a multitude of ailments.

Douche Bath

A powerful icy jet was directed at the ailing parts of the patient. Where the water pressure was inadequate, a high overhead tank was used. Dr Wilson's tank at Malvern boasted a drop of 20 feet, which necessitated the wearing of protective headgear by the patient.

Unfortunately these supposed cures could also result in nasty accidents like that of the woman who stood on a chair to reduce the drop – the water pressure was so high that it actually broke the chair. Another example is that of the gentleman being treated in the Douche in winter, who was stabbed in the back by an icicle.

The Man / Woman Issue

There are several widely acknowledged differences between the sexes. Women mature faster than men. Women, as a rule, are more ready to admit their emotions, and have a longer life expectancy than men. However, one of the most enduring differences between the sexes lies in what they keep in the bathroom and how long they spend in there. Not wishing to make sweeping generalisations, one can rest reasonably assured that the average man will have a toothbrush, toothpaste, razor, shaving cream and a bar of soap in his bathroom. Oh, and he might run to a towel. A woman, on the other hand, may have up to 459 items – most of which will be unidentifiable by a man.

Many domestic arguments arise from men getting frustrated at how long their partner spends in the bathroom. I suppose one reason for this could be

105

that women have so many objects in bathroom it takes them forever to find the one they are looking for.

In response to the enduring question of whether toilet seats should be left up or down, Lucy Prentice from Vancouver has written an ode to toilet seats.

Love

When a wife will wash

her husband's back

Then get a towel from off the rack,

That's love!

And when at night he warms her feet,
Although he shudders
When theirs meet,
That's love!
Or when she makes his favourite cake,
Though the day is far too hot to bake,
That's love!
But of all the signs depicting love,
There are few that can compete
With the man of the house remembering to
Put down the toilet seat.

This clearly provides much useful insight into the question that has plagued thinkers ever since the dawn of time, or the dawn of toilets, anyway. However, as Lucy herself points out, why would a lid have ever been designed if it were not meant to be used? A toilet is not the most attractive of utensils, and closing the lid considerably improves its appearance. Moreover, shutting the lid prevents household pets drinking out of it and toddlers from throwing things inside it. And, quite honestly, there are more pleasant things to look at than the inside of a toilet bowl when cleaning one's teeth at the basin adjacent to it.

'There won't be any revolution in America,' said Isadore. Nitkin agreed. 'The people are all too clean. They spend all their time changing their shirts and washing themselves. You can't feel revolutionary in a bathroom.'

Eric Linklater, Juan in America

Western Bathrooms

You can tell a lot from a bathroom – it reflects the way of thinking of the country and its people. The most telling sign is how the toilet or bathroom is referred to. In Britain, W.C. stands for water closet and is a very apt euphemism in true British style. The water closet is a modern word for the privies found in medieval castles. Bathrooms are also referred to by a number of other names – toilet, loo, cloakroom, dunny, bog, kazi, little boy's room. Many people give their own pet name for the bathroom, which is probably the only room in the house that receives this special attention.

In 19th century America, 'the smallest room in the house' was spoken of in hushed whispers. Today they politely call it the 'restroom'.

The Italian 'bagnio', however, could not be more different. Going back to the Roman baths where males and females bathed together and showed absolutely no concern about doing so, the tiny Italian 'bagnio' of today sports neither a shower curtain nor a door, which means that it is impossible to have a shower without drenching everything else in the bathroom. The Italians do not seem unduly worried about the concept of dripping towels.

In Ireland the problem is how to turn on the shower and even once this hurdle is overcome, the problems are only beginning. The Irish bath sports knobs with inner and outer dials and sometimes a separate on/off switch just to complicate matters. Ireland's quaintness and individuality is born of the fact that no two Irish baths are the same. Of course, this helps the Guinness trade considerably, as approaching the whole rigmarole after a pint or four may make things seem clearer, but it cannot be denied that travelling in Ireland presents complications where one would least expect them.

Of course, the opposite problem may occur and not being able to turn the shower off may be distinctly more embarrassing. Running down to the reception of your hotel or to the manager of your campsite or to the warden of your youth hostel clad only in a towel, hair dripping, could be a trifle awkward, especially if you do not speak the language.

Naturally, Swiss bathrooms do not pose the remotest logistical problem, because everything in Switzerland runs like clockwork anyway – efficiency is the name of the game. The rail system, the pocket-knives and the minutely observed precision watches are only the tip of the iceberg. As well as being superhumanly efficient, Swiss bathrooms are also extraordinarily clean. Stray hairs never find themselves in Swiss showers. Swiss towels are probably the smallest and the thinnest in Europe, just so as not to waste a square centimetre of space.

Most of us will have experienced the delights of using a French toilet: a hole in the ground which you have to balance over precariously, whilst trying to swat the flies that are buzzing around you and trying to work out how the French manage without any toilet paper. For such a sophisticated nation their lavatorial facilities leave a lot to be desired.

In my experience, if you have to keep the lavatory door shut by extending your left leg, it's modern architecture.

Nancy Banks-Smith,
The Guardian, *20 Feb., 1979*

The Toothbrush

The origin of the toothbrush is unknown, although dental hygiene has been a priority for many centuries. Indeed, the very worst insult that can be offered in the African Congo is to accuse someone of not having cleaned his or her teeth. For this purpose, the natives of that country carry willow twigs with frayed ends wherever they go.

When Queen Elizabeth I died, her teeth had changed colour from their original rather fetching yellow to an even more fetching black. Reports from that time would suggest that the most effective way of preserving one's teeth was by means of a linen cloth which one could rub around the inside of the mouth. Another means was in the form of 'Vaughan's Water' of 1602, an advertisement for which billed itself as doing 'much good for the head and sweeteneth the breath.'

Lord Chesterfield advised his son in 1754 to clean his teeth with a sponge and lukewarm water. Other popular recipes for dental care included soot (which may have been where Queen Elizabeth went wrong), nettles, tobacco, ashes, honey, pulverised nuts and fish bones.

Soap

Soap was not introduced into England until the 14th century, 'toilet waters' being used before its introduction. The first soaps were usually home-made, and indeed, one diarist wrote that her 'myrrh water' was:

'good to make on lok younge longe; I only wete a fine cloth and wipe my face over at night with it'.

'Bauer's Head and Bath Soap' was advertised in the 1880's and claimed to be a first-class shaving soap. However, this appears to be something of a contradiction in terms, as it was also promoted as encouraging the growth of hair.

The use of soap was actively discouraged during the reign of Oliver Cromwell, who introduced a 'soap tax'. During the early 1700's there were over sixty soap factories in London. Soap became more than just a cleansing agent: an advert for 'The True Royal Chymical Washball' claimed that apart from ridding the skin of all 'Deformities, Tetters, Ringwoem, Morphew, Sunburn, Scurf, Pimples and pits or redness of the Small Pox' it was warranted to 'give an exquisite edge to the razor, and so comfort the brain and nerves as to prevent catching a cold'.

One can be far more imaginative with bathing than simply using soap and water. Indeed, history has a fine record of those who have washed in milk. Poppeia, the wife of Nero, never went anywhere without her train of sea-asses to produce a steady supply. William Douglas, the 4th Earl of Queensbury, also bathed in milk, and apparently used to try to seduce pretty girls by making this fact about his ablutions well known. The fact that he died unmarried is perhaps not altogether surprising.

As well as milk, baths have also contained pine needles, seaweed, vats of wine (which could be fairly blissful), camomile, thyme, rose petals, walnut leaves, nettles, oak bark, and even chlorine and hydrochloric acid.

Chlorine and hydrochloric acid apart, the above may carry romantic and/or seductive connotations with them, but just to balance them out, baths have also been known to contain peat, blood and horse manure. Eskimo women are said to bathe in their own urine.

Stage celebrity Cora Pearl was reported to have bathed in champagne, and ladies' magazines of her time advocated hock and claret as a superior form of shampoo. Its superiority goes without saying, although us lesser mortals may have to resign ourselves to sticking to the supermarket variety.

Other Books from Summersdale

More Chat-up Lines and Put Downs
Stewart Ferris   £3.99

How To Chat-up Women (Pocket edition)
Stewart Ferris   £3.99

How To Chat-up Men (Pocket edition)
Kitty Malone   £3.99

Enormous Boobs
The Greatest Mistakes In The History of the World
Stewart Ferris   £4.99

The Romance Book	£5.99
Classic Love Poems	£5.99
Words for Women	£5.99
A Book of Inspiration	£5.99

Girl Power
Kitty Malone   £3.99

The Kama Sutra For One
O'Nan and P. Palm   £3.99

101 Reasons Not To Do Anything
*A Collection of Cynical
and Defeatist Quotations*   £3.99

How To Say 'I Love You'
Stewart Ferris   £4.99

Available from all good bookshops.